Humor Love Sex Beauty—these things make the inevitable suffering in life bearable. ... Pragmatism and function have their spheres, but this sphere is well understood by

1. TEMPTING DISASTER

I began to research disaster in spring 2019—one year before today's pandemic, economic chaos, an uprising, and ash falling gently from orange Western skies.

I was responding to a call for artists to work with a coalition creating an outdoor community hub for disaster preparedness on the campus of Portland State University. Around the table were public-interest designers, university and municipal emergency management, and a private energy company. Portland has a one in three chance of suffering a major earthquake in the next fifty[1] years, and quake preparedness was the main focus of concern.

Although I had lived through the 1989 Loma Prieta earthquake in San Francisco, I've had many other disasters on my mind in more recent years, ones that affect us every day depending on who we are and where we live: the housing crisis, escalating inequality, and the climate crisis. I've been thinking about the connection between personal crisis and public crisis, what interpersonal and emotional resources we need to respond effectively, and how artists engage with these issues.

I've come at these things from many different angles, both as an individual and as a collaborator with grassroots groups—storytelling, interrupting traffic, mutual aid work, eviction defense, art installation, political graphics and participatory performance. After a lifetime of outsider cultural work and advocacy, I wanted to learn how insiders approach big, overwhelming problems. I wanted to know how they create large-scale and longer-term strategies at a safe distance from a "future" event.

At the time, I was heavily influenced by Rebecca Solnit's book *A Paradise Built in Hell*. The book describes how traditional emergency management, and most of our blockbuster movies, are based around the belief that in the wake of disaster, chaos ensues. Systems break down, individuals fight for resources, and authorities need to manage the situation through strong central control. Solnit describes numerous examples of what actually tends to happen on the ground: everyday people seek connection, self-organize and practice mutual aid (with the caveat that this mutual aid can take oppressive forms, for instance, racist vigilante neighborhood groups).

Solnit also describes the surprising yet common presence of joy and humor in this self-organization—an element distinctly missing in institutional response. And she marshals modern, evidence-based disaster research to support her argument.

---

[1] https://www.newyorker.com/magazine/2015/07/20/the-really-big-one

The people planning a disaster prep hub in Portland had this same research in mind. Committee members wanted the hub to become an everyday community gathering spot, both to visibilize preparedness and to ensure that people would spontaneously gather there in the event of a big disaster. They wanted artists to help draw people to the site. I started thinking through what I could offer. What could an artist do that a giant institution could not?

The context for this work has shifted radically since that beginning, over and over. Therefore I'll approach this as a story, zig-zagging and leap-frogging, while continuing to wind around and around a central question: *what is the role of art in urgent times?*

I dug into how disaster lives in our pop culture, how we carry the idea of it around in our daily lives, and how we prepare for the worst—or don't. I spoke to emergency managers and activists involved in mutual aid work. I interviewed public health nurses who run role-playing games to give social workers some taste of what it's like to navigate social services. I dug into emergency management literature and looked at historical European depictions of "Apocalypse."

At the time I had just emerged from a series of personal losses. Those losses had inspired a participatory mail art project, exploring the intimate networks of care that sustain us through individual and collective grief. Applying this lens of care, I considered the gaps in the existing toolkit of emergency management. It tends to stay focused on the rational and material world—logistics, command centers, radio beacons, water storage, electrical grids, go bags. Yet, conversations made clear that a clearly-explained educational pamphlet is insufficient to convince regular, already-overwhelmed people to take basic steps to prepare for disasters that aren't yet affecting them personally or feel too big to grasp.

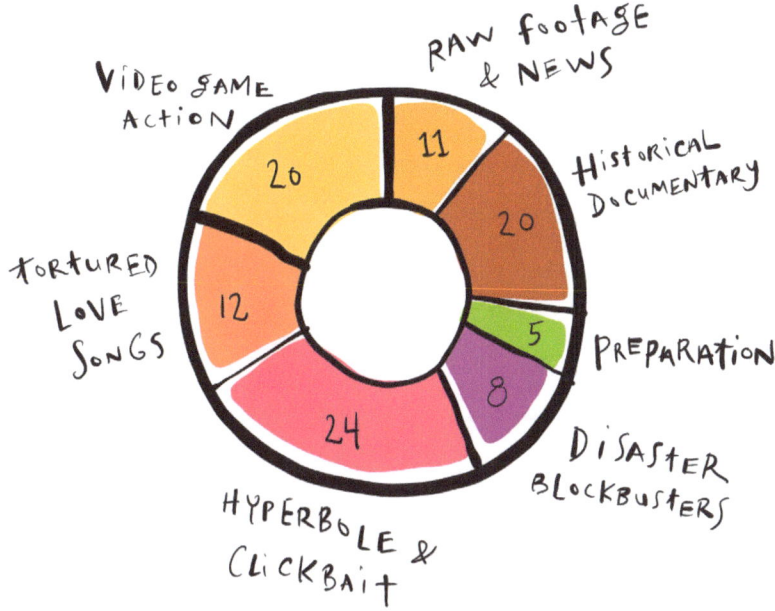

THE ARTISTS' EMERGENCY RESPONSE CYCLE **3**

I wondered what could happen if we asked people how they *feel* about disaster, not just how they *think* about it, or how many gallons of water they have stored away.

As part of my research, I tried small-scale experiments and tested tabling on campus. I asked people about what a safe place might look like for the kinds of disasters that they dreaded in their own lives. I also made a six-minute mashup of excerpts from the top hundred online videos whose titles contained the word "disaster"—ranging from actual disaster bystander footage, to informational videos, to Hollywood disaster movies, to pop songs about romantic breakups. Then I asked people to watch it and take a Disaster Response Test, recording positive and negative emotional responses, and talk to me afterwards about their experience.

I used all these conversations and interactions to brainstorm a spring series of public events on the site of the new "Prep Hub." Staff, faculty, students and neighbors together, to build community ties, to spark expansive dialogue about crisis and disaster, and to practice concrete collaborative survival skills with humor and creativity. Togetherness builds resilience.

The universe had other plans. ■

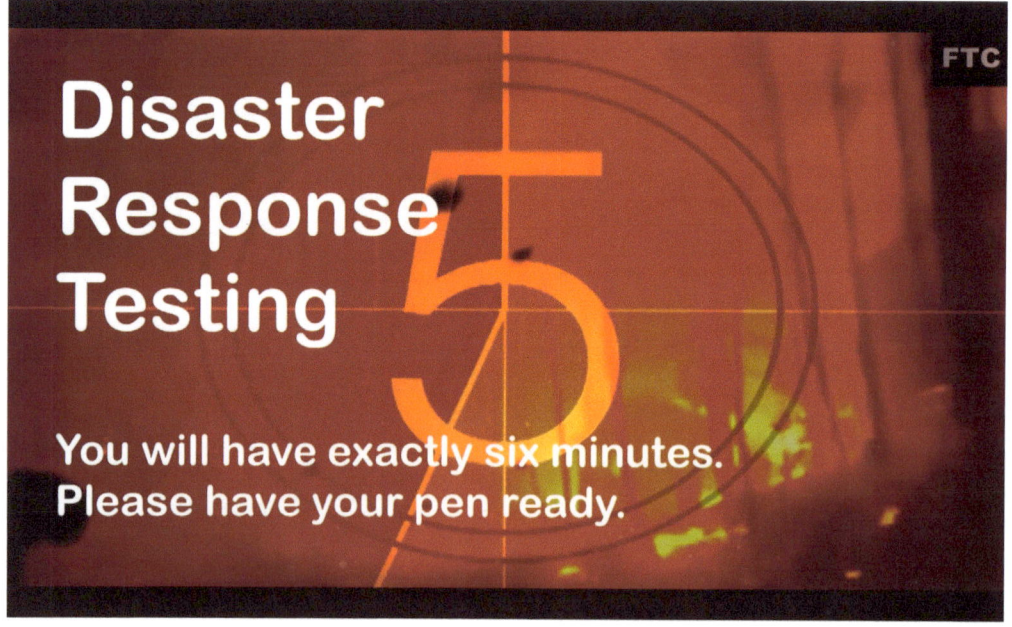

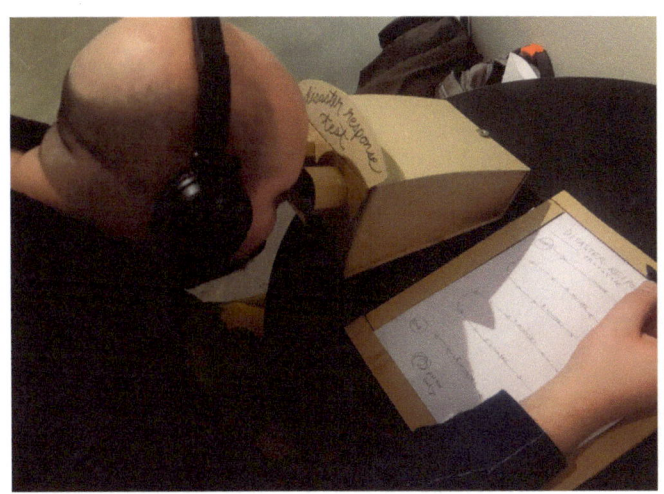
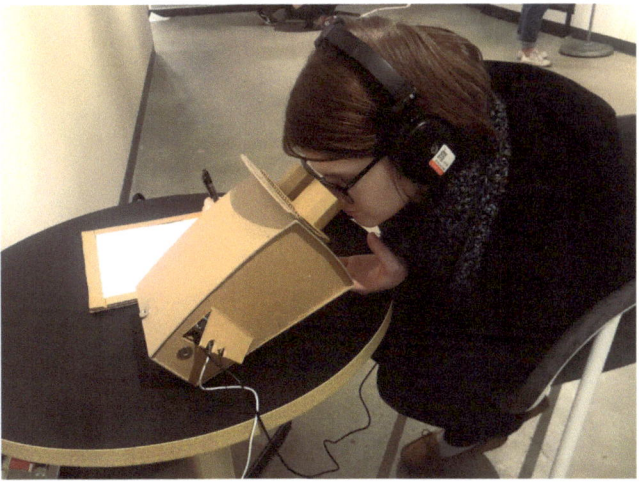
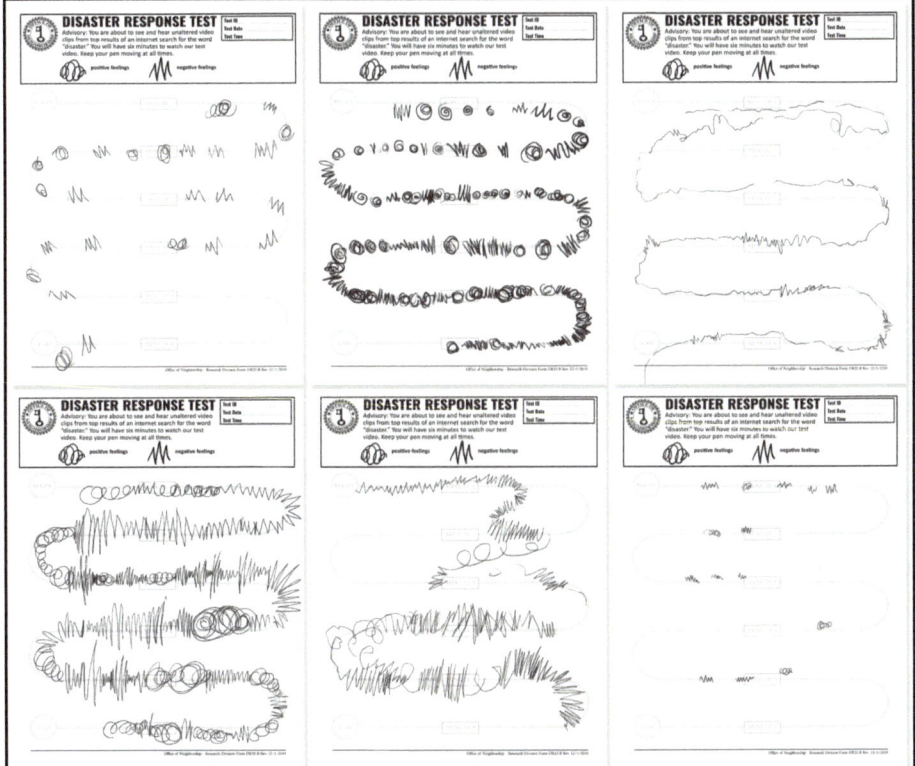

Students at Portland State University take the Disaster Response Test.

"Advisory: you are about to see and hear unaltered video clips from top results of an internet search for the word 'disaster.' You will have six minutes to watch our test video. Keep your pen moving at all times."

THE ARTISTS' EMERGENCY RESPONSE CYCLE

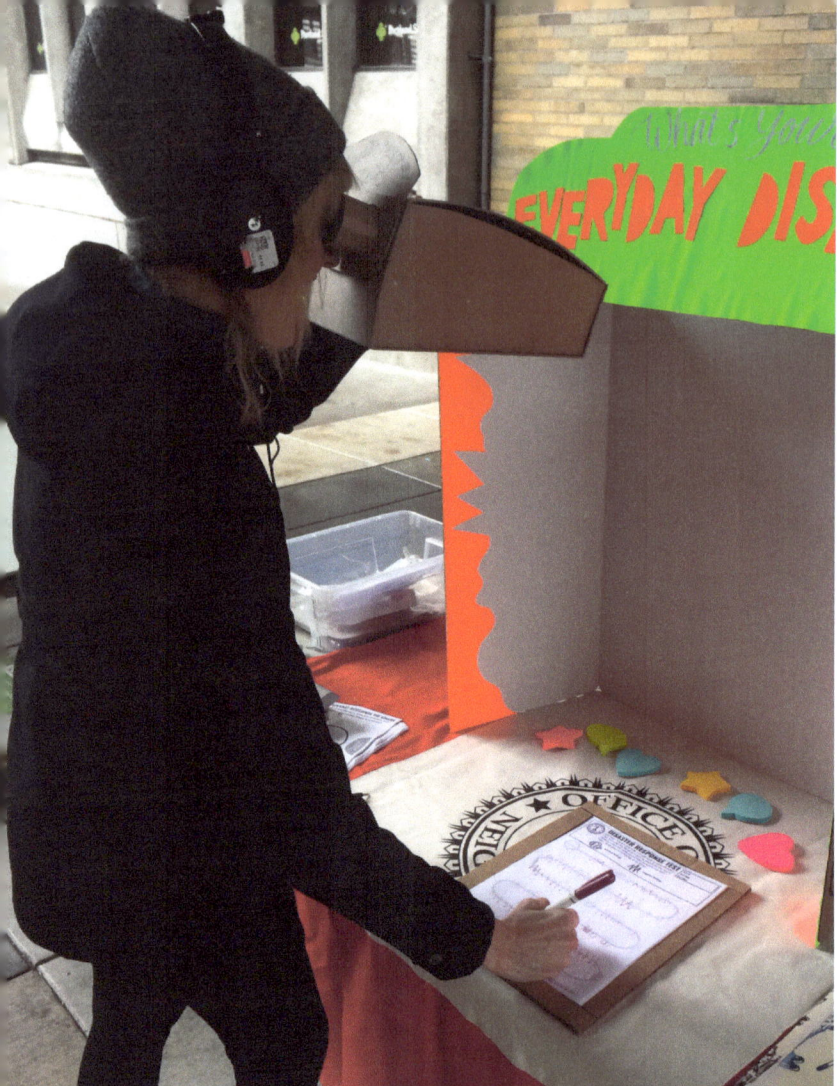

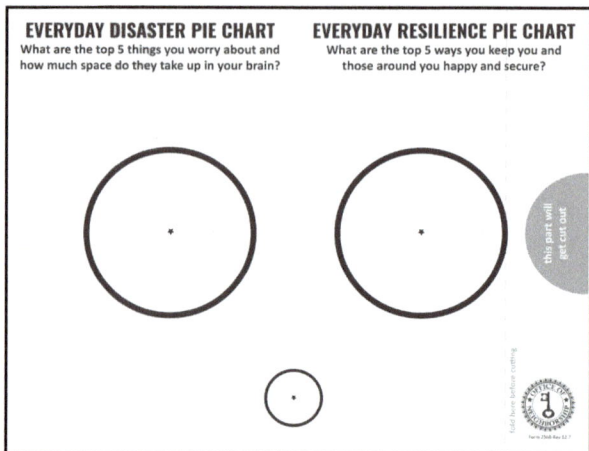

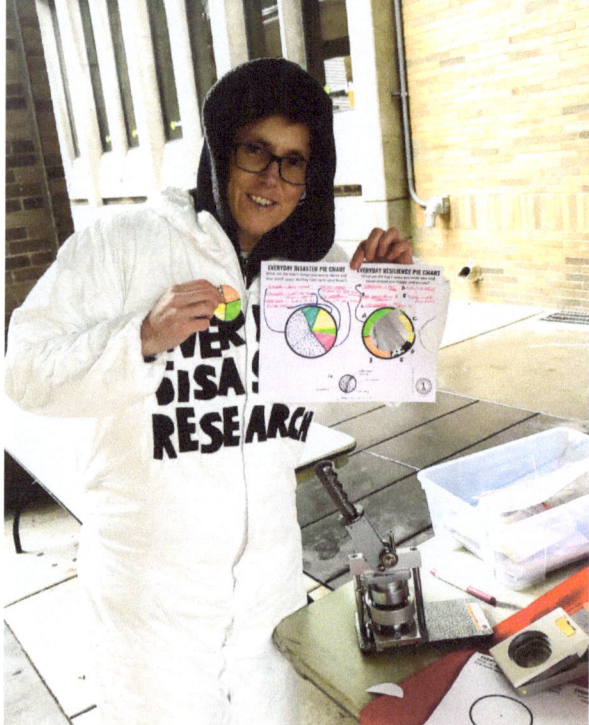

Tabling on campus at Portland State University, with the Disaster Response Test and an Everyday Disaster / Everyday Resilience Pie Chart survey. I provided participants with an instant button diagramming their responses.

CHATS ABOUT DISASTER

We can't predict disasters, but we can predict the state's response. In the wake of disaster, how can we reconstitute in a more liberatory way, rather than regressing to the status quo or being bulldozed by "disaster capitalism" and rightwing forces taking advantage of the chaos to make radical advances in their own agendas? ... Part of disaster preparedness is building your relationships with people who are already having a hard time.
—Eva Irwin, Rosehip Medic Collective

I'm a little sympathetic towards this odd tendency of the individual survivalist. Like, if as an individual I know how to help other people survive, then that's the only thing that will get us all through. Like, I know CPR. I know how to make beef jerky. I know X, Y, and Z thing. I can't rely on the people in charge because they don't seem to be worried about anyone other than themselves. ... Maybe part of the fantasy of being prepared for something terrible is that I'm not actually prepared for the smaller disasters that might happen.
—Mary Olin Geiger

I have had up close experiences with hardcore addiction in my family. I'm a lawyer, but my brother is living in a tent right now. And it feels overwhelming, like wow I got nothing for this, I don't know what to do—which is how global warming feels to a certain extent right? We can do catastrophe planning for an earthquake or a forest fire or gas leak, that's one thing. But some things are so big and so ongoing and so deep that you can't figure out where the point of the fulcrum is.
—JM

LOVE DISASTER DANCE PARTY

EMERGENCY MEAL KIT COOK-OFF

DISASTER MOVIE MARATHON

EVACUATION DRILL DORM DANCE ROUTINE

DISASTER BOARD GAME NIGHT

SEISMOLOGY interpretation CONCERT

GO KIT CONTEST

Activity proposals for the site of the community disaster preparation hub. Thanks to Emma Stocker of PSU Emergency Management for her suggestion of an Emergency Meal Kit Cookoff.

2. SLIPPAGE AND RESPONSE

As I was fleshing out plans and reaching out for collaborators, I occasionally wondered if the Big One might arrive while I was running some Disaster Movie Night or training. Instead, as we all know, the pandemic rolled in and slapped us sideways. It was suddenly dangerous to touch or speak to another human being at close range. Projects, calendars and morale collapsed like so many unreinforced masonry buildings in an earthquake. The disaster "Prep Hub" got put on hold, and members of the committee turned to more immediate emergencies. Campuses emptied. People lost their jobs. Hunger spiked. The acute disaster illuminated and exacerbated the already-ongoing crises of economic and racial inequity, and the inadequacy of government response.

Volunteers sprang into action, as in the wake of every disaster, in both practical and visionary ways. They started fundraising, they jump-started mutual aid networks to distribute essential supplies with creative workarounds to keep people safe. Many artists, including me, participated in these efforts. Many people exhausted themselves with this work. I continued working with the PDX Trans Housing Coalition, as I had been for several months, but my efforts moved from a budding "Surviving with Dignity" zine project to direct deliveries of essential supplies.

Many people, including me, also spent too many hours stuck at home, staring at screens, obsessively reading frightening headlines, straightjacketed by the risk of other people and of public spaces.

I wasn't moving my body enough. I was feeling jittery, unfocused, and upset. This seemed to be a common condition. How could we snap out of it? It was one thing to stack another box of soup and diy hand sanitizer at the local distribution point, or deliver a C-PAP machine to someone living in a car. But how could we apply emotional first aid in this situation, so I and people around me could maintain enough equilibrium to keep rising to the occasion? How could we shake off the paralysis and helplessness that are the basic building blocks of trauma? What could mutual aid for the spirit look like?

So I organized an outdoor dance party. ▪

3. THE EMERGENCY DANCE PARTY NETWORK

This may seem contrary, but in fact, many people started hosting dance parties—on Instagram, and over Zoom, and Twitch.tv. Many were people who already worked in dance and music. For me, my unprofessional urge came from my early adulthood experience of moving to San Francisco, an epicenter of the AIDS crisis, as AIDS deaths in the US were starting to spike up towards 100,000.[1] The Christian Right was using the disease as a lever point to further exclude and demonize LGBTQ+ people. Queer folks were already dealing with homophobic discrimination in housing and employment, street violence, family rejection, high suicide rates, plus the fear of this deadly disease.

People responded in all kinds of ways. They/we took care of sick friends and lovers, demanded accelerated research, and protested homophobic laws and institutions. But they also wielded the powerful tools of performance, art and participatory culture. They/we created spaces for storytelling, play, and exchange, and created new narratives that made it possible for queer folks to survive and thrive.

Performers put on campy and outrageous safe sex demonstrations in nightclubs. Saving lives wasn't just a practical matter of showing people how to put a condom on a banana. These shows celebrated the full gamut of risky sexual practices, not just the ones considered acceptable for a government-funded pamphlet. They showed cheering patrons how to use safe sex supplies, and they also made it feel sexy. To this day, the knowing snap of a latex glove still

Chalk circles delineating safely-spaced dancing zones at the first Emergency Dance Party at MLK Jr School

[2] https://www.amfar.org/thirty-years-of-hiv/aids-snapshots-of-an-epidemic/

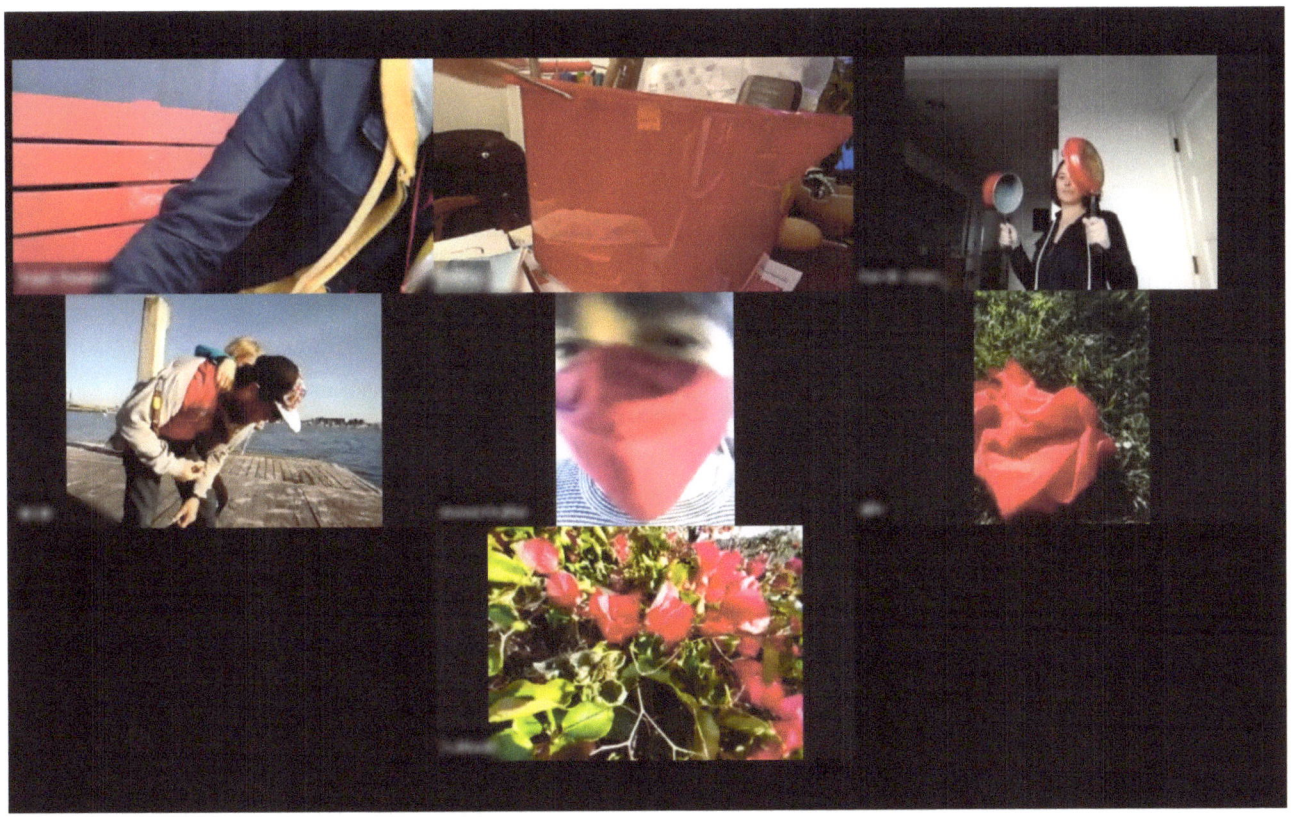

Screenshot of online participants in the Emergency Dance Party, dancing with something red

means something good is about to happen, with no risky downside.

So in dialog with the evolving demands of quarantine, I wanted us to practice new physical-distancing behaviors to take care of each others' health in the context of a deadly virus. And I wanted to do this alongside the basic first aid of connection, motion and play. I made this happen by drawing on my extended network of friends, acquaintances and co-conspirators. Ariana Jacob's emphatic 'yes!' sparked the first Emergency Dance Party out of an imaginative space and into concrete form. She recruited DJ Seamstress of Sound, who brought beats appropriate to the times.

We chalked out fourteen circles in a parking lot in NE Portland. We created the circles as a visual marker and reminder for the dancers— to help us retrain our bodies to maintain a six foot distance.

(continued on page 15)

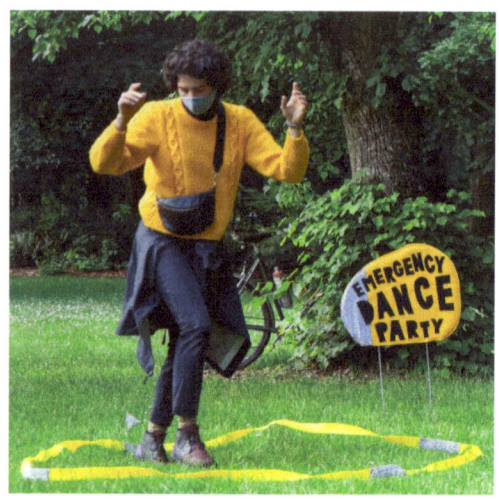

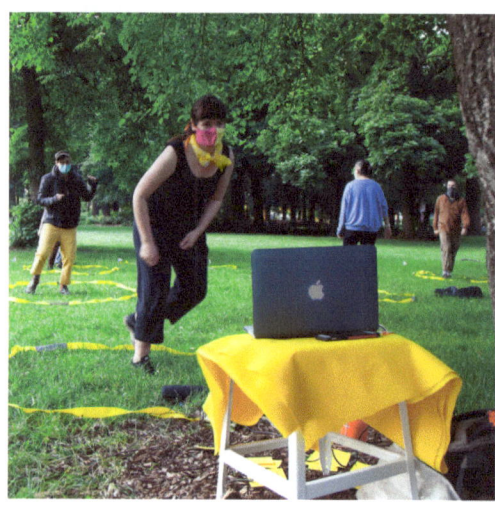

Emergency Dance Party in Alberta Park

Photos by Emily Fitzgerald

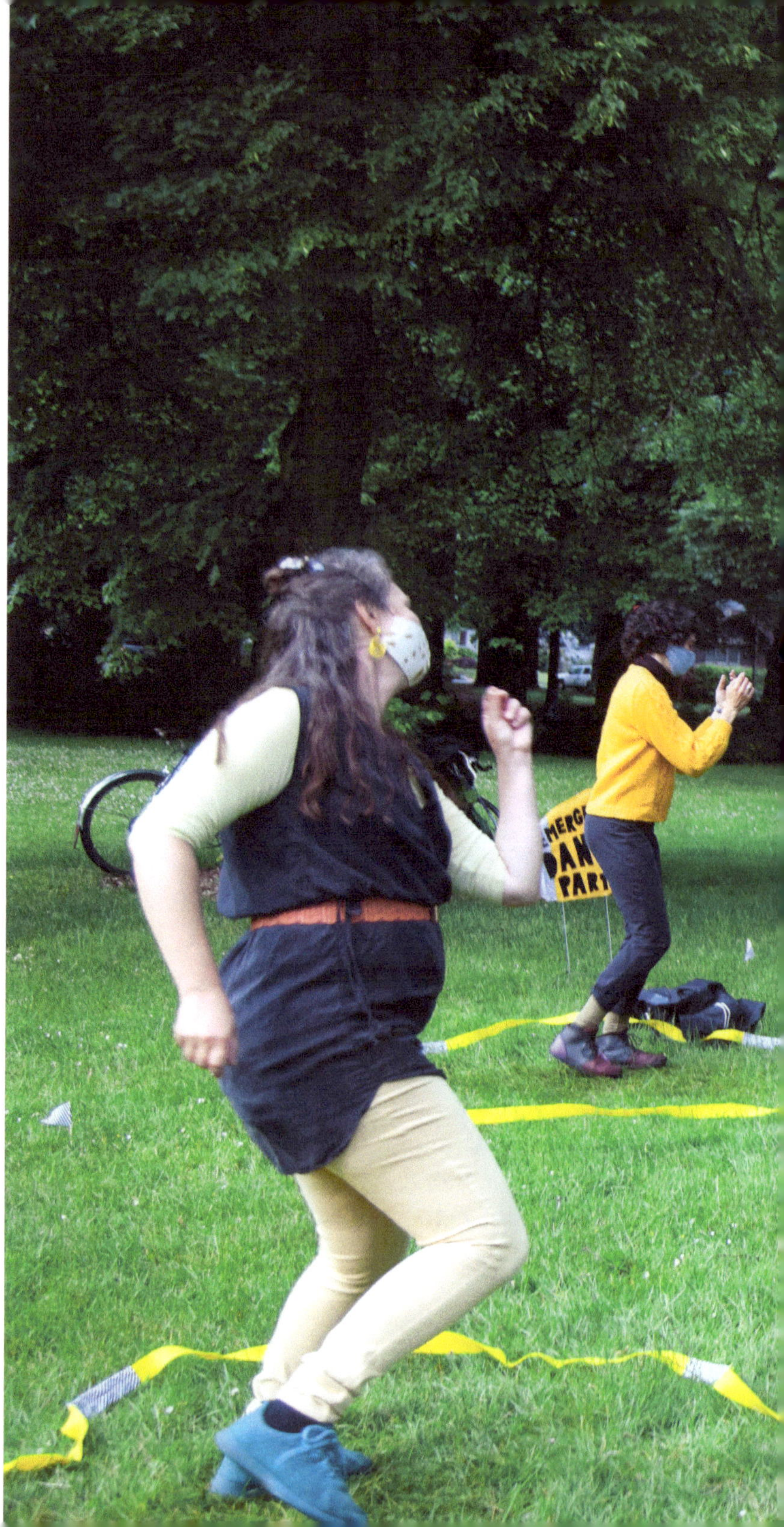

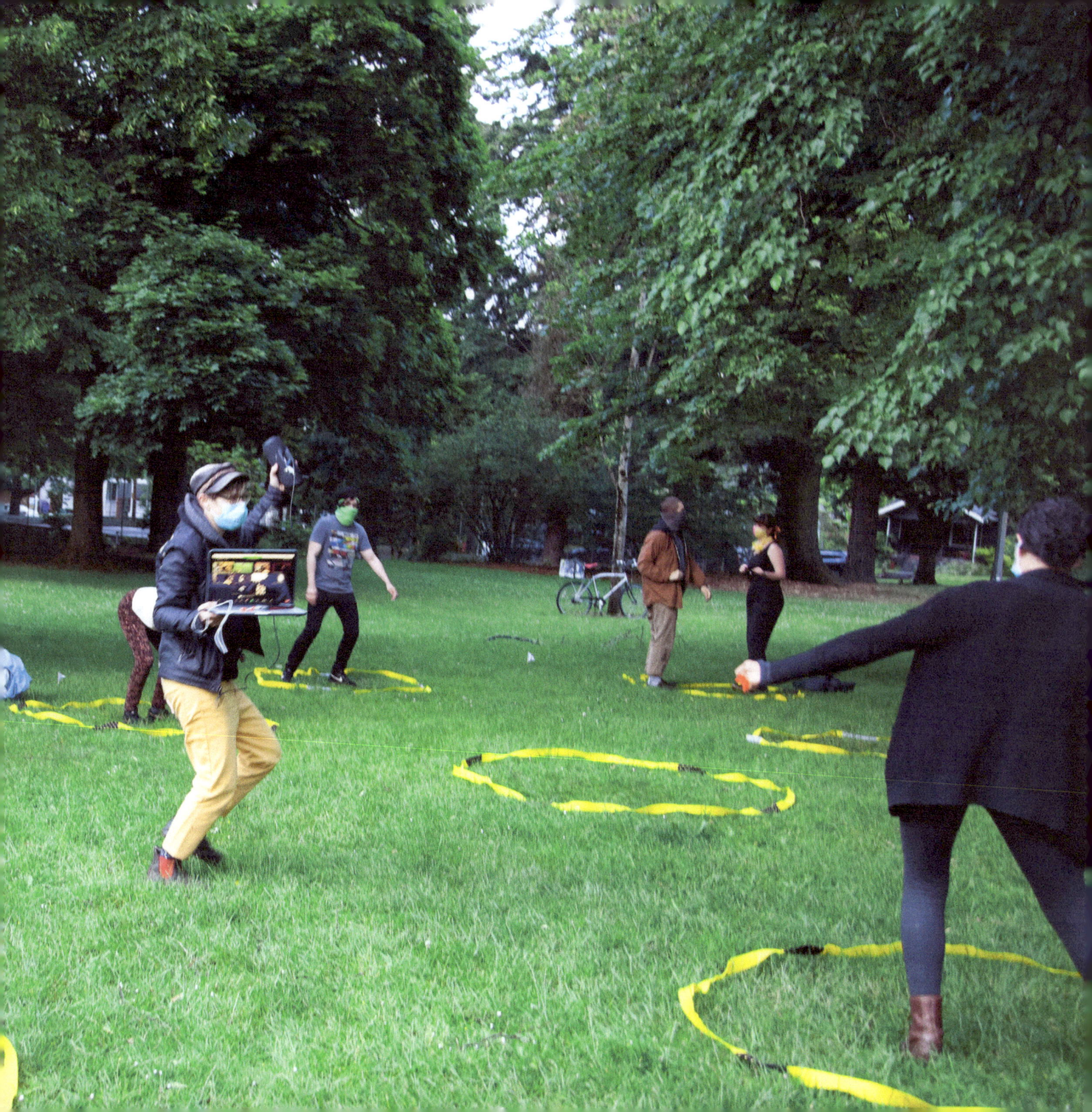

CHATS WITH EDPN PARTICIPANTS

Those first few weeks I definitely felt really activated and scattered. Time was really weird and hard. ... When I first saw the invitation I thought, no way do I want to be in public dancing. I'd be so embarrassed. But then my favorite part ended up being dancing outside. I felt like I was doing something for the world by just being silly and being outside.
   —Ammi Keller, dancer, Oakland CA

We're all feeling a little bit squirrelly. ... You're having this experience, and how can you draw in other people to help support you through that experience? We get to benefit vicariously from helping you get through your emergency. I loved doing that first one when my daughter and I got up on Bernal Heights. There was this family of two dykes and two kids, an older toddler and his sister was maybe five or six. I was dancing, and they weren't. This little kid was just looking at me like crazy. And I said, it's a dance party with friends in other states! And the two women were both like, cool! And he started dancing along by himself as he walked by.
   —Anne Williams, dancer, San Francisco CA

There are a lot of people questioning how we can reshape culture and politics now. Your project is a form of play and joyful experimentation towards this idea of having the skills to respond politically in a different way. I want so much more of that. It's not practical. There's still a giant gap between how you do this thing and then how you actually make a political movement happen. But we need joyful experimentation even not knowing how it's going to actually create results.
   —Ariana Jacob, dancer & collaborator, Portland OR (pre-uprising)

(continued from page 11)

We also created the circles to help passers-by and neighbors understand that we were being safe, and to make our practice visible as a possibility for other folks seeking creative workarounds for isolation.

Through these collaborators' networks, we gathered a distanced crowd. Dancers arrived in various states of anxiety, curiosity and relief, and smiled as they moved. And many more people joined us through Zoom, from as far away as Singapore, the Yukon, and the Eastern US. People seemed excited to take a break from the other ways they had been responding to the pandemic (whether that was coordinating relief, caring for kids, defending vulnerable people, moving work online, or maybe just spending the day curled in a panicked ball around their cellphones.)

This coming-together echoed one major conclusion of disaster researchers: that communities with existing strong ties fare best in the wake of disaster. (Even if, in this case, the community was partly virtual.)

Portland's mayor declared shelter-in-place two days later, and the Emergency Dance Party moved to a weekly all-virtual format for a while. I experimented with online meeting technology, encouraged people to dance outside if possible, and came up with creative movement prompts that people could do in their backyards, kitchens and public parks. After the infection curve flattened, and people seemed more comfortable with sharing outdoor space, we resumed in-person dance parties using handmade felt hoops that could be spread out at a distance anywhere. ■

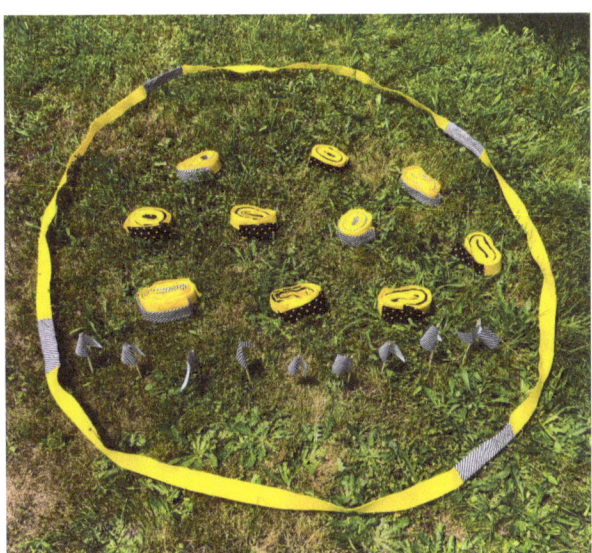

Portable felt hoops and flags for the Emergency Dance Party

4. EVACUATION ROUTES

As the weeks went on, there was continual disorientation and whiplash from ever-changing information about risk factors, mask wearing, how to take care of our essential needs, where to find toilet paper or make substitutes. Lots of people I talked to were feeling shut down, overwhelmed, and out of their bodies. The dance parties were keeping me in balance, but I wanted to get beyond basic first aid. How could we cut through the overload, take detailed stock of our surroundings, clear our heads and start to re-imagine a future? Could a participatory art project help with that too?

Portland's shelter-in-place order made an exception for outdoor exercise, so I restlessly walked, biked and danced all over the city, sometimes while in an online class, meeting or workshop. I began listening to Janet Cardiff's pre-recorded audio walking tours[1], which confuse past and present, here and elsewhere, fiction and reality, in ways that resonated with the weirdness of moving around in the world with twenty people on my phone.

I also observed that social behaviors in "public space" were morphing daily, in the crossfire of emerging science, cultural norms, and a powerful drive towards togetherness. I started paying close attention— if I had a dog, would I have more legitimacy as I wandered? If I averted my eyes at close quarters, like many people did, was that really lowering my chances of transmitting a virus? If I stepped off the sidewalk and faced fully away from another pedestrian, would that be interpreted as a caring gesture or an unfriendly one? What felt safe to touch?

I wanted to explore this with other people, so I started experimenting with a guided walk via

---
1 https://soundcloud.com/incredibleworksofart/sets/janet-cardiff

THE ARTISTS' EMERGENCY RESPONSE CYCLE

Zoom, leading people on "evacuation routes" starting at their own front doors and exploring the internal and external minutiae of their journeys. Where did they want to walk and why? Who did they encounter? How did it feel? How could we share glimpses of our multitudinous geographies?

Then, George Floyd was murdered, and the mandate of "don't leave your house except to exercise and get groceries" clashed explosively with a mass uprising declaring that racism is as much of a public health risk as coronavirus. Public space shifted drastically again as thousands defied shelter-in-place to march side by side through the streets.

In this kind of head-spinning context, we need to find ways to navigate besides automatic pilot. I heard about the OODA Loop while listening to a podcast featuring Queer Nature, a couple running a nature education and ancestral skills program serving the LGBTQ2+ community. OODA stands for Observe-Orient-Decide-Act, and the loop is a decision-making tool developed by a military strategist for uncertain and chaotic environments. Basically, you practice using your senses to closely observe local conditions; then you apply intellect to interpret what you've observed; then you make a decision about your next action; then you act; then you observe again.

I decided to see what happened if I appropriated the OODA Loop into the guided walk. Instead of focusing on rapid decision-making, I slowed the cycle down. I also added a fifth step, a crucial one when we are practicing not only our literal next steps but the next steps for transformed communities. The fifth step is the artist's secret sauce, imagination.

THE ARTISTS' EMERGENCY RESPONSE CYCLE **17**

The walk looped through these steps:

We started with **Observe**, or "where are we?" I asked participants to slow down and pay attention to the details of what was happening in their own bodies and what was happening around them when they left their homes. I asked them to observe colors, temperatures, sounds, smells and textures. Close observation calms our nervous systems and gives us important information.

Then I had people **Orient**, or consider and interpret what they were noticing— both in the external world and in their own choices as they walked along.

I asked people to **Imagine** what was around them that they couldn't observe directly. They invented a companion animal for their walk, considered the intangible and made unusual moves in public space, as a way to get unstuck from limitations and hypervigilance and expand the possibilities for creative decision-making.

Finally, I asked participants to **Decide** and **Act**—to consider options for safety and risk, such as whether to walk towards other people or away, and whether to touch interesting things they came across.

Many people experimented with me on early versions of Evacuation Routes and offered insightful feedback about how it felt to move through public space in this way, navigating distant directives that rubbed up against social norms, performativity, neighbor relations, racial boundaries and the particularities of their local landscapes.

The culminating event involved participants from two colliding virtual events: City Repair's Village Building Convergence, which brought walkers from the sustainable living community, and Assembly, an annual program of workshops and talks organized by PSU Art and Social Practice students.

Walkers shared their observations with their phone cameras and microphones, and could scroll through to see what other participants were sharing. Shawn Creeden live-mixed a gorgeous accompanying soundscape, including audio clips from pandemic-stilled public spaces, recorded on request by collaborators around the globe.

The resulting video and audio recording was a moving mosaic of glimpses from multiple places at once, complete with all the stutters and imperfections of cell networks. Only fully visible as documentation after the event, it produced a collective impression of a unique convergence of space and time. ■

CHATS WITH EVACUATION ROUTES PARTICIPANTS

If you live in dense spaces, you work out a physical connection where you're almost not acknowledging other people because you're just letting people do their own thing, in proximity. But now we actually have to negotiate proximity. We're trying to build a new physical vocabulary that we can actually use to communicate these social intentions.
   —Gretchen Till, walker, Oakland CA

What was so magical about it for me was having someone else guiding this sensory experience ... I can take a route I've taken many times and experience it very differently. I did different things because of the prompting. I went towards more people. I went into a mostly Black neighborhood. And then I felt self conscious about being this [white] weirdo clearly doing an art project—self-conscious about touching anything, and very aware of the freedom I felt to claim my presence. There were so many things I wanted to point my camera at, but I couldn't hold my phone up towards somebody's front door in a neighborhood where I'm seen as a threat.
   —Mary Doyle, walker, Gainesville FL

I've been stopping and smelling flowers. A lot. And touching the things it feels safe to touch. And I'm really curious about the texture of it and the temperature of it and the shape, because I haven't been able to touch another human being in two months. I went and slept on the beach outside of town for a couple of nights. I just need to go touch things and plants. Dirt. Rocks. Water. You know what I mean, just to feel alive.
   —MB, walker, Portland OR

EXCERPTS FROM THE SCORE FOR EVACUATION ROUTES

Point your finger in the direction of the nearest place to get water. Point your camera in that direction so we can see your hand pointing. Point your finger in the direction of the nearest hospital. Point your finger in the direction of someone you miss. Point your camera in that direction. If you don't know how to answer, point the camera at the sky.

...

What kinds of boundaries are shaping which direction you go? Are there invisible lines you can't cross? If they're invisible, how do you know they're there? See if you can cross one of those invisible lines and take a new direction.

...

Find something red. Fill the lens of the camera with it. Let's wait until everyone finds something. OK point your camera at your feet again and keep walking.

...

Where is the closest police station? Point your finger in that direction. If you don't know where it is, point your camera at the sky. Is that a safe place for you to go? Is that a dangerous place for you? Where is the closest safe space for you?

...

Why do you want to touch this thing? If it feels safe and possible, touch it. If you can't touch the thing, just continue to share it with us. Let's just record this together for a moment, remembering what it's like to touch things.

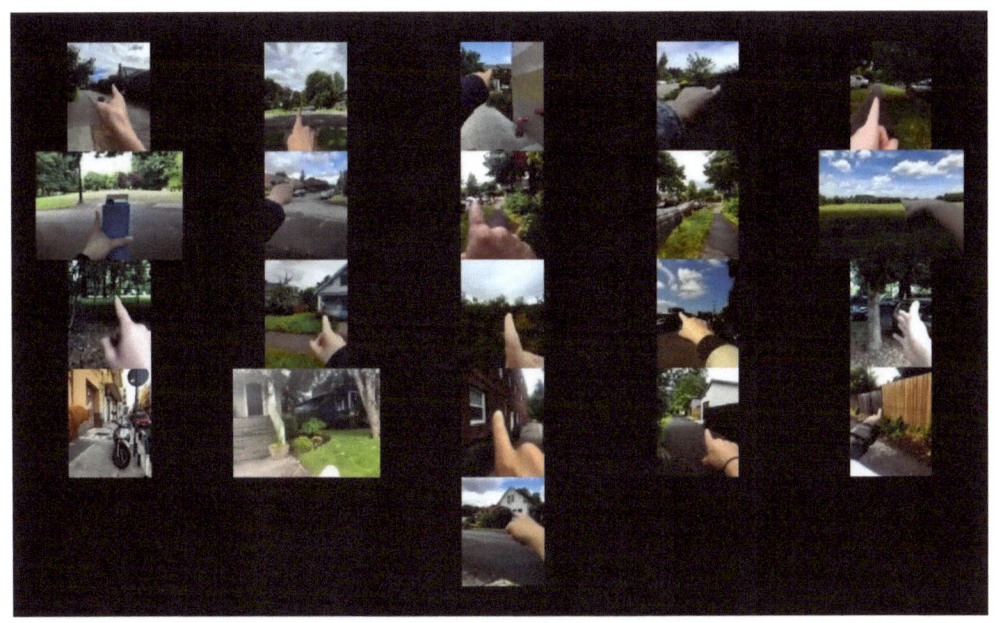

Still image from Zoom recording of Evacuation Routes: point at the nearest source of water; find something red

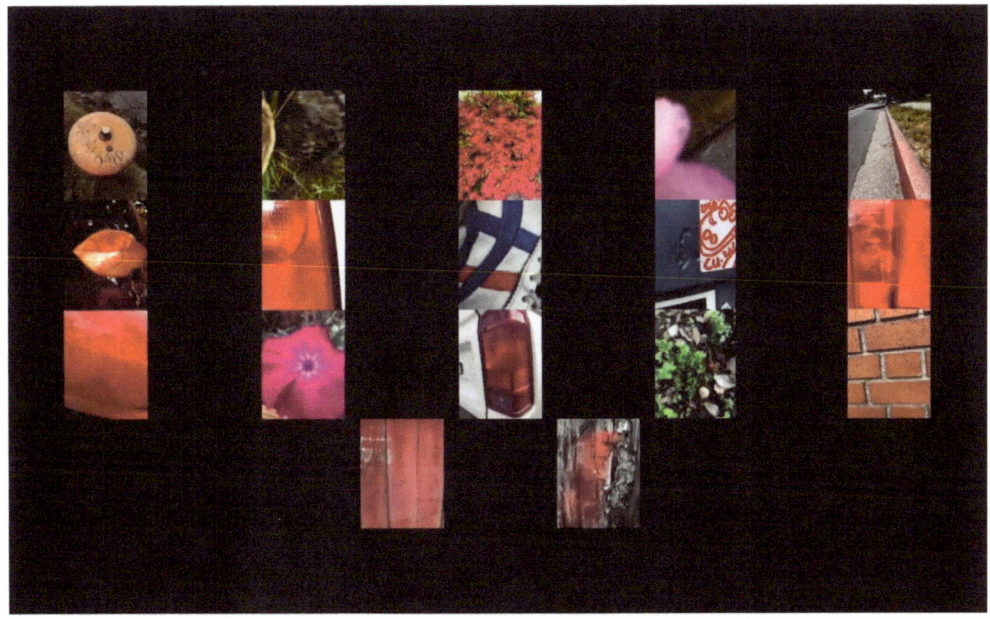

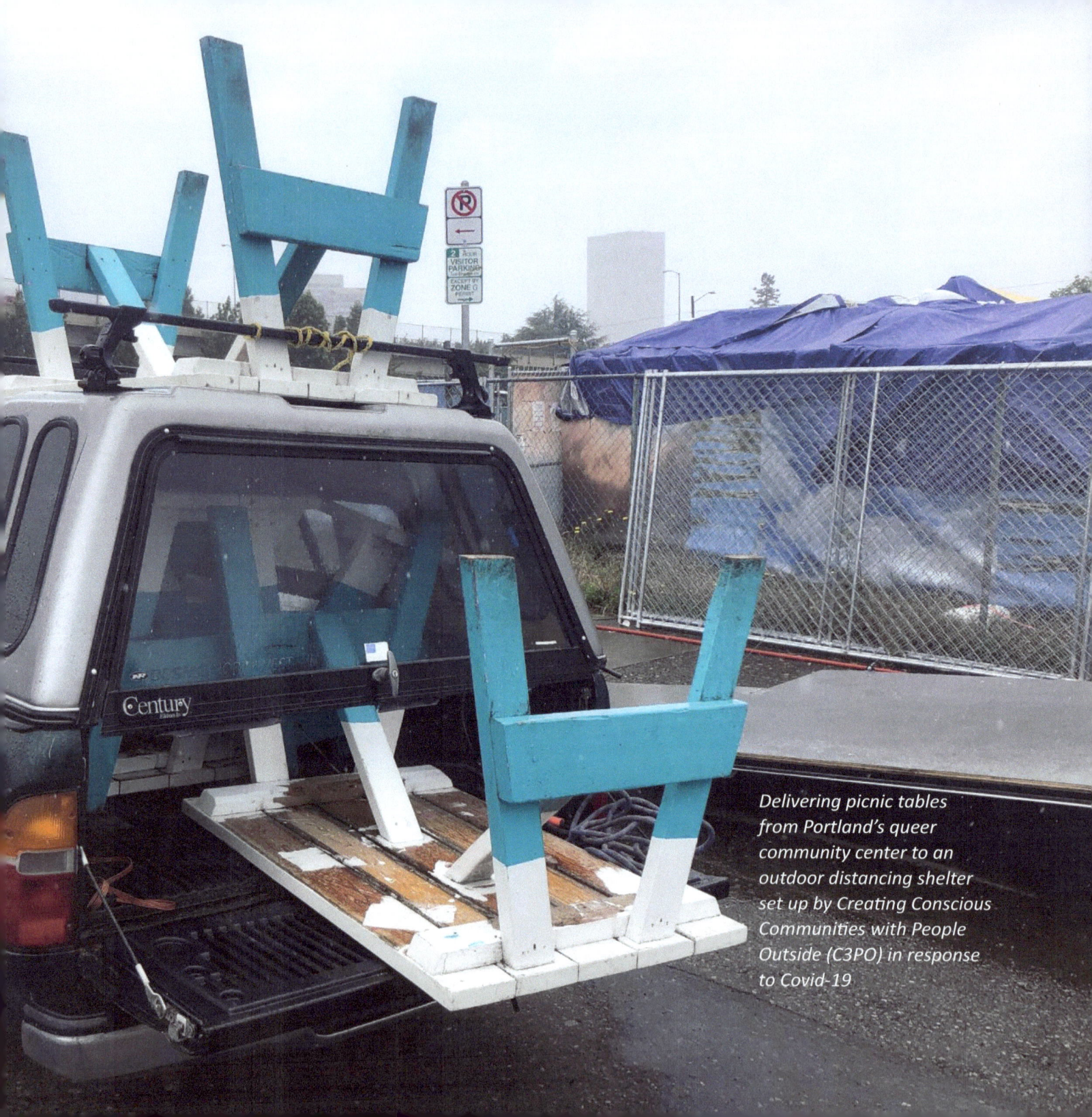

Delivering picnic tables from Portland's queer community center to an outdoor distancing shelter set up by Creating Conscious Communities with People Outside (C3PO) in response to Covid-19

5. SHTF[2]

I was working with the PDX Trans Housing Coalition and allied housing organizers to source tents and other supplies for Portland's emergency outdoor distancing shelters when the national uprising over racial injustice erupted. In this context, the Emergency Dance Party Network and Evacuation Routes projects felt both personally uplifting and also utterly inadequate.

This moment hit right at the heart of my question about the role of art in a crisis. In my work with grassroots movements addressing economic justice, climate change, racial justice and their intersections with queer liberation, I have used both artistic and activist approaches. In theory, these approaches could be complementary. In practice, while political graphics and agit-prop sometimes close the gap, the open-ended approaches demanded by contemporary art aren't usually seen as relevant in activist spaces, and goal-oriented social justice strategies often land with a thud within the arts.[1] Activists value simple, clear, accessible, and declarative projects that create an immediate real-world impact. Art offers room for contradiction, intimacy, and questions that endlessly generate more questions, in ways that feel hard to justify when SHTF.[2]

Why dance when people are shutting down police stations and lining up at food banks? Why walk slowly and pay attention when it feels like we can't possibly keep up with everything we need to do and know? What possible role do these kinds of intimate projects play within this big, overwhelming picture?

Here I'll cycle back to my original question, and make it more specific: *"How can participatory art strategies support our collective resilience in the face of escalating and overlapping crises? What is the role of play, ambiguity, and open-ended questions in addressing social, political and environmental urgencies?"*

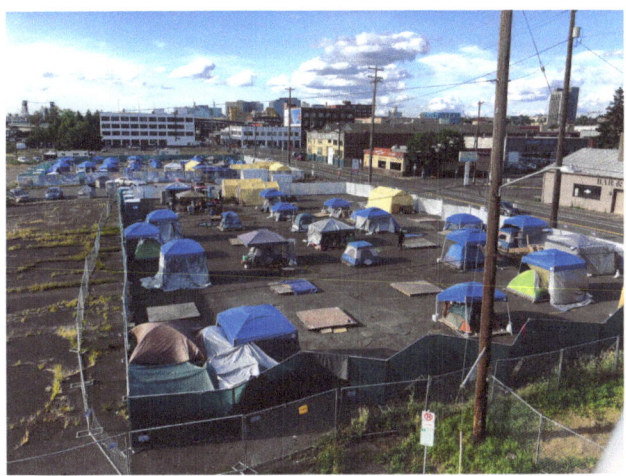

Queer and BIPOC affinity camps set up by Creating Conscious Communities with People Outside (C3PO)

---

1   I often look to the Center for Artistic Activism for wisdom on this topic
2   Shit Hits the Fan, a common acronym among survivalists

THE ARTISTS' EMERGENCY RESPONSE CYCLE

I suggest that artists facing similar questions consider another practical institutional diagram. The standard emergency planning cycle describes different phases of action in the face of disaster.

In this framework, **Response** is a time for first aid, or stopping immediate harm—bringing concrete resources and relieving symptoms so people can hold themselves together and coordinate baseline necessities.

Recovery is a phase of rebuilding and getting 'back to normal".

Mitigation aims to make long-term, large-scale and infrastructural shifts that reduce the likelihood and severity of disaster. In emergency management, Mitigation might mean changes in how and where we build homes, or how communities are organized, or what we're putting into the atmosphere.

Preparation accepts that some disasters will continue to occur, and tries to get individuals, communities and institutions ready to respond to them.

All well and good. Artists can and do engage in all these approaches. So do activists. But what's missing here? What is the special and unique contribution of the arts, and in particular, artists that engage community?

On the following page I describe some of the metaphorical hammers, saws and chisels in the creatives' toolkit. None of these approaches are universal, and anybody can use them. But many artists prioritize these things, practice these things, and get good at these things.

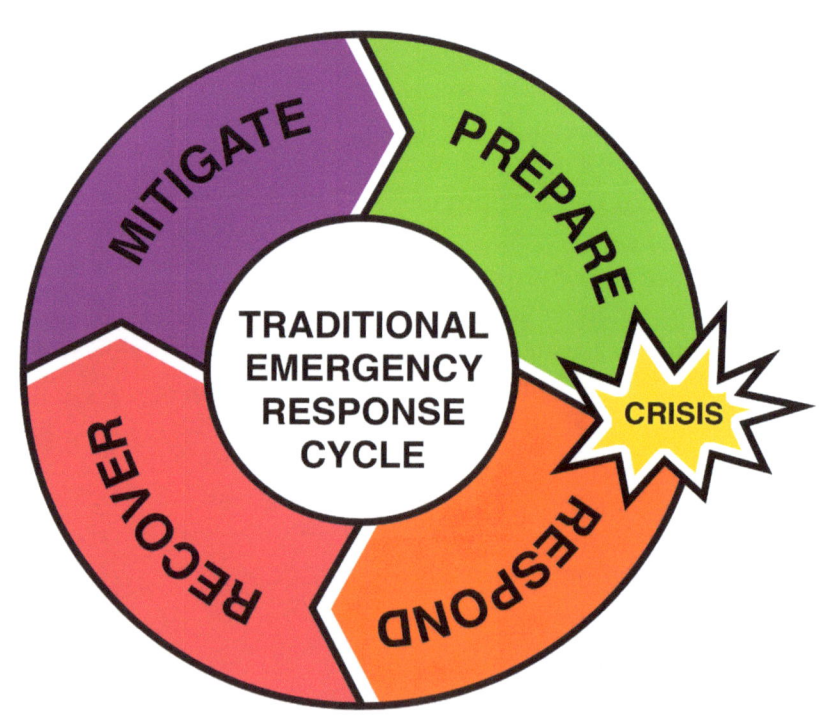

THE EMERGENCY TOOLKIT OF THE ARTS

Art allows the emotional, the irrational and the intuitive. It tends to be organic, spontaneous, and responsive.

Art can bring curiosity, experimentation, play or humor into unlikely situations.

Art uses multiple modes of learning and observation. Art remixes disparate languages, specialties, impressions and ideas, and produces unexpected outcomes.

Art is willing to upend accepted frameworks, step across invisible lines, and break rules to get to a more complex truth. Art can use a space or a technology or a concept in an unconventional way.

Art seeks open-ended answers, and can imagine rearrangements of the most mundane aspects of our daily lives. What if this parking lot was a tent village? What if this parking lot was a dance floor? What if we could find ways to resolve conflict without police?

Art can push conversations forward, discovering loopholes and escape hatches from conceptual dead ends.

Art can create something that never existed before. ▪

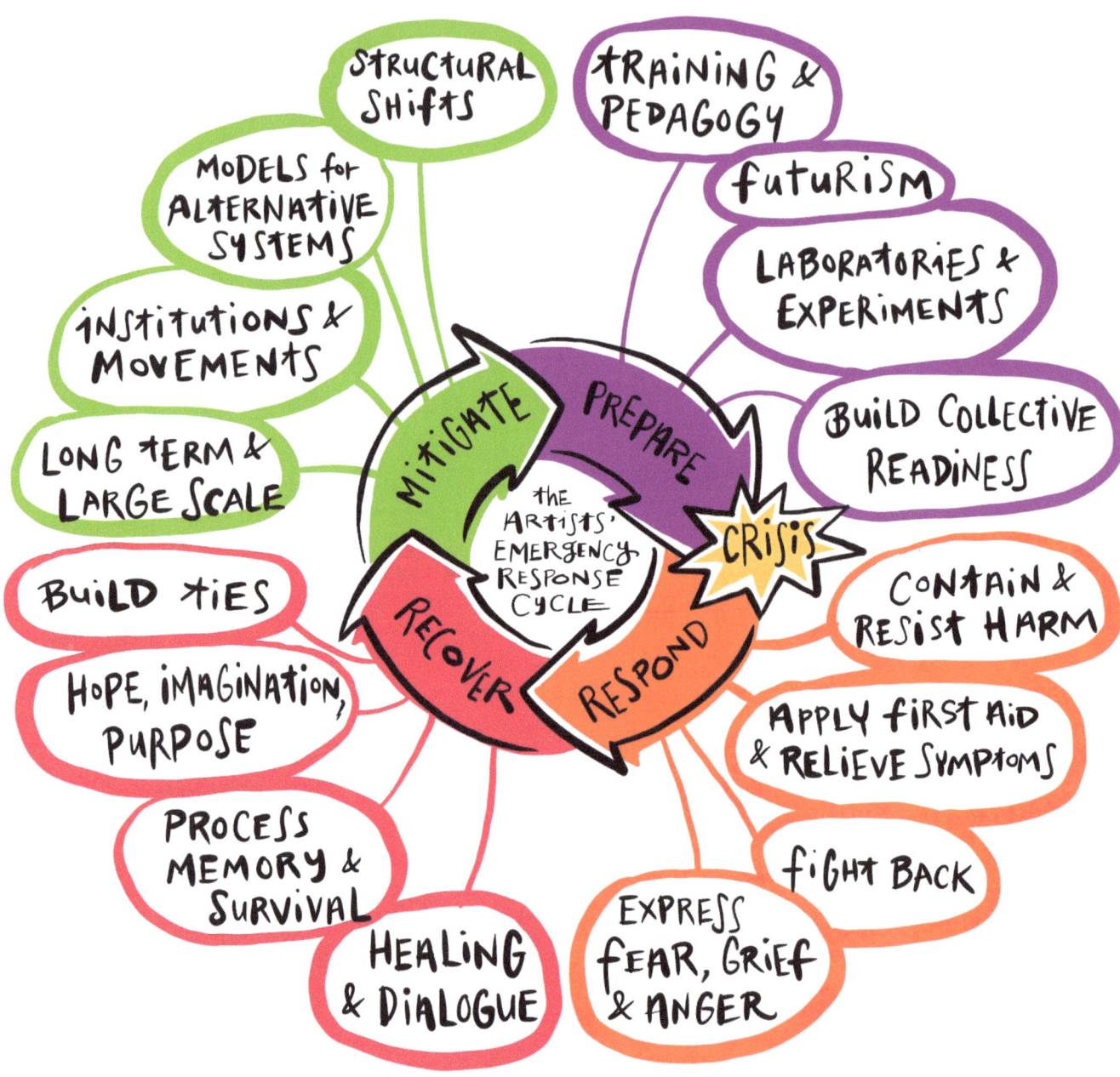

6. THE ARTISTS' EMERGENCY RESPONSE CYCLE

I'd like to propose a parallel cycle that suggests ways for socially-engaged artists to contribute their specialized strengths to the collective well-being amidst escalating disasters.

Because these crises are often overlapping and systemic, the choice of which of the four steps to focus on might depend on each person's location, focus, and vulnerabilities. In many ways they are strategies more than phases. We might call this "diversity of tactics," with many points of entry. With this perspective, let's go back through the cycle, while considering some socially-engaged art projects that might model each phase.

RESPONSE

"Response is a phase for containing harm and applying first aid—bringing concrete resources, relieving symptoms and establishing baseline coordination of necessities."

The art of Response is often "quick 'n' dirty" and straightforward, made efficiently when time, energy and materials are in short supply. In the case of social disasters, "containing harm" can also mean fighting back against harmful systems. A key word here is "anti-."

Creative protest and agitprop are common forms of Response practiced by visual and performing artists in direct collaboration with social movements. Cannupa Hanska Luger, for instance, designed mirrored shields for Standing Rock to reflect security forces back to themselves and protect protesters from physical attack. Plenty of artists have also used activist strategies to interrupt crises of systemic inequity within art world institutions, including the Guerrilla Girls, Global Ultra Luxury Faction (GULF), Liberate Tate, and xsfmoma. Ai Wei Wei risked beating and imprisonment to tirelessly petition the Chinese government to release victims' names from the 2008 Sichuan earthquake.

Humor, satire and irrationality can be powerful forms of Response as well. The Dada movement insisted on passionate nonsense in reaction to the bleak, rational absurdities of the first World War. The Clandestine Insurgent Rebel Clown Army used clowning, humor and non-violent tactics to participate in direct action against corporate globalization, war, and other issues, while challenging preconceptions of what a radical activist looks like.

Artistic Response can also acknowledge emotional impacts. It can create space for the expression of fear, grief, or anger in reaction to a harm, or provide emotional first aid. In this framework, the Emergency Dance Party Network and 90s-era safe sex performances were simple Responses to the immediate need to stop viral transmission, but they also combated isolation and overwhelm. In the last six months, people around the globe have come up with interesting ways to do both, creating physical gathering spaces divided via athletic field markings, Plexiglas partitions, even pool noodle hats.[1] Artists who painted political murals on boarded-up storefronts during this summer's racial justice uprising reflected and energized the protests in the streets, and created a powerful visual backdrop for media accounts.

RECOVERY

Recovery is a phase of rebuilding and getting "back to normal".

In the Artists' Emergency Response Cycle, Recovery is a healing and dialogue phase. However, emergency management's language around getting "back to normal" enshrines a status quo that is often far from desirable for many people. So, Recovery in this framework is about meeting people where they're at, processing memory and survival, gaining full access to feeling, and connecting with hope,

[1] https://thetravelintern.com/social-distancing-around-the-world/?amp

imagination, humor, purpose, and community ties. So much queer art that came out of my community in the 90s served this role—storytelling, image-making and dancing our way out of invisibility, rejection, trauma and violence, regenerating a sense of wholeness and belonging. Within the overwhelming context of shelter-in-place, Evacuation Routes stepped in this direction —bringing participants' full faculties online through the OOIDA Loop, practicing our abilities to observe, orient, imagine, decide and act as one part of a collective body.

This is the most common role for socially-engaged art addressing crisis—many, many artists do this work.

To name a few: Tricia Hersey's ongoing Nap Ministry project practices rest as resistance to capitalism and white supremacy—"rest as our foundation to invent, restore, imagine, and build." The Black Life Experiential Working Group's 2019 HERE || Humboldt centered a Portland neighborhood's Black life of the past, present and future, and employed a Social Emergency Response Center (borrowed from Design Studio for Social Innovation) to make space for collective information-sharing, idea generation, and creative response to community ruptures. In 1988, Guillermo Gómez-Peña and Emily Hicks staged a Border Wedding on the Tijuana-San Diego borderline, with poets and musicians performing on both sides, and family and friends making unauthorized crossings during the ceremony. Suzanne Lacy's

2018 Across and In-Between collaborated with communities on both sides of a different border, the one between Northern and Southern Ireland—interrogating "a line on a landscape" and its profound impact on people living alongside it during a time of intense international focus around Brexit. Ghana Think Tank sets up laboratories in so-called 'developing countries' to help solve first-world problems. AA Bronson's recent A Public Apology to Siksika Nation attempts to grapple with familial culpability for settler-colonialism and cultural genocide. And Jon Rubin and Dawn Weleski's Conflict Kitchen served the food of countries in conflict with the US, to spark dialogue and engagement across political lines.

MITIGATION

"Mitigation aims to make long-term, large-scale and infrastructural shifts that reduce the likelihood and severity of disaster."

Mitigation work demands a high level of commitment and organization. Here is where artists, designers and creative thinkers/doers of all kinds work to restructure the building blocks of our culture, create replicable models for alternate systems, shift power, and influence baseline policies and norms. In this realm, occasionally an individual artist can create a viral new idea, but most commonly, this is where we will have the most impact through learning to collaborate with social movements, networks and institutions who can leverage social and financial capital.

At the level of Mitigation, some obvious examples are Rick Lowe's Project Row Houses in Houston and Theater Gates' Rebuild Foundation in Chicago, as well as Jeanne Van Heeswijk's work with Homebaked Bakery and the Homebaked Community Land Trust, among many other projects. Mel Chin's Operation Paydirt/Fundred Dollar Bill Project leverages community engagement and art to lobby the US Congress to address lead poisoning. Caroline Woolard created online barter platforms Trade School and Our Goods as "systems of interdependence" to enable collaboration and mutual aid. Cassie Thornton worked with Strike Debt to create Rolling Jubilee, a project that bought and eliminated almost 38 millions dollars' worth of debt, and is currently experimenting with The Hologram, a "viral, peer-to-peer feminist health network." The US Department of Arts and Culture appropriates the trappings of a government agency to connect artists nationally and "devise cultural policies and programs to catalyze profound culture shift in the service of social and environmental justice." Working Artists and the Greater Economy (WAGE) works to establish better pay and labor conditions for artists and create more equity in the arts economy.

PREPARATION

"Preparation accepts that some disasters will continue to occur, and tries to get individuals, communities and institutions ready to respond to them."

Preparation shares many features with Recovery—the building of individual capacities and community ties—but it is focused on the future more than it deals with the past. This work has strong pedagogical, organizing and visioning components that get us ready to act effectively in future crisis.

Sometimes the efforts are experimental one-offs. Rosehip Medic Collective and Faultline Theater Ensemble's 2014 Holding Onto the Sky placed audience members in the middle of a community meeting coping with the aftermath of a major earthquake in Portland, OR. Justin Langlois's 2016 Academy of Tactical Resistance was a "pop-up education zone for the radicalization of everyday practices and adjustments… [to] support the resistance of the small, the porous, the invisible, and the routine." Stephanie Syjuco's 2017 Speculative Dissent Laboratory experimented with protest signs, street actions, and documentation/dissemination to search for new visual languages and tactical strategies for disruption. The Radical Imagination Gymnasium exercised the muscles of the radical imagination through a collaborative exhibition, workshops and workouts using various means to develop collective visions of our present and the future.

Some of these projects look like ongoing organizations or initiatives. The Center for Artistic Activism brings artists and activists together to cross-pollinate their skills towards more effective advocacy work. The Center for Cultural Power, a successor to Faviana Rodriguez and Jeff Chang's Culture Strike, works to co-create cultural strategy with organizations and artists through trainings, convenings and design teams. Jeanne Van Heeswijk's Trainings for the Not-Yet is an ongoing series of trainings in "civic engagement, radical collectivity, and active empowerment, bringing together collaborators from various fields and communities to create and practice alternative imaginings of being together in the face of the pressing emergencies that shape the world today." The Laboratory of Insurrectionary Imagination has a long history of working in this mode. In 2015 they held a series of hackathons and trainings culminating in the Climate Games, the world's first "Non-violent Civil Disobedience Direct Action Adventure Game" coinciding with the protests at the Paris COP21 Climate Summit. Tania Bruguera's Immigrant Movement International, sited in a multinational neighborhood in Queens NY from 2010-15, created an educational community space, an immigration think tank, a lab practicing activist tactics, and a place to encourage immigrant communities to maintain and celebrate their roots while adapting to U.S. culture. ■

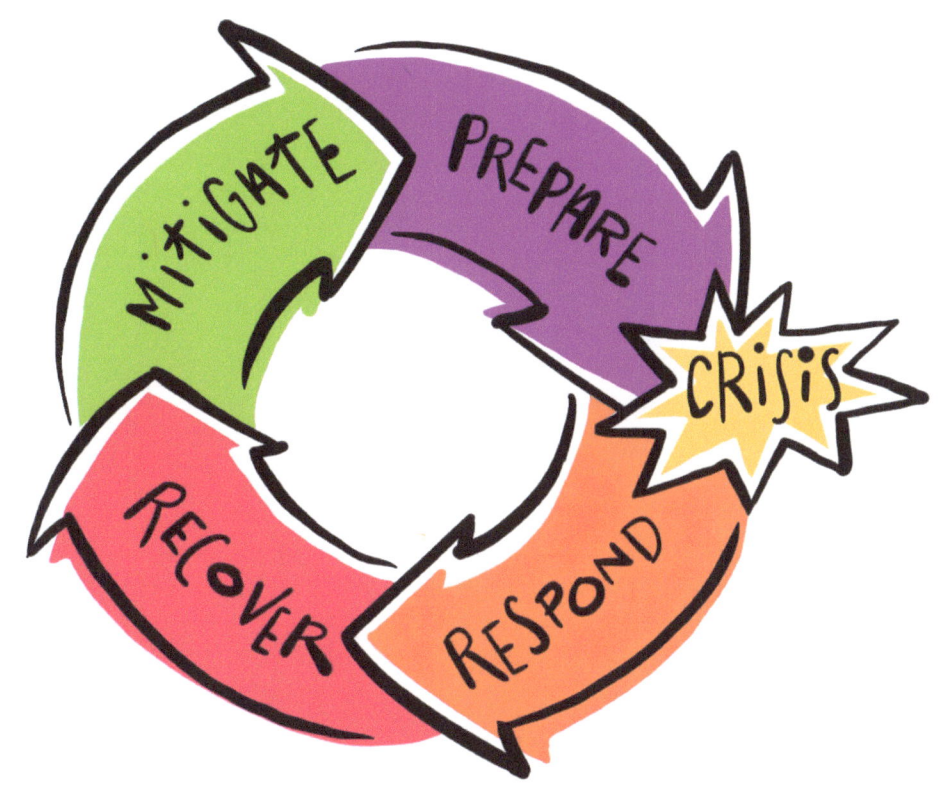

**NOW IT'S YOUR TURN!
SPIN THE WHEEL!**

7. WRAPPING UP

I began this research as an experiment in bringing art strategies to a collaboration with institutions focused on Mitigation and Preparation. As the pandemic struck, I drew on my strong suits: re-starting the cycle of Response and Recovery, focusing on the crucial grassroots network- and community-building at the heart of both collective crisis response and social practice work. I am continually aiming towards Mitigation and Preparation, and continually cycling back to the necessities of Response and Recovery, and around and around we will go.

All of these approaches are needed, at some times more than others. All of them can include play, ambiguity, and the kind of open-ended questions that start conversations rather than finish them. In that vein, I'm curious what other artists and cultural workers think of this framework. Good art often transcends and remixes categories, so please feel free to argue with me about which projects belong where. There are also many powerful, meaningful projects that don't directly address crisis or fall neatly into this scheme. But I hope the Artists' Emergency Response Cycle is helpful as a lens to ask what a project is actually *doing* in relationship to a problem.

We are in times of great urgency, and multiple demands on our energy and attention. How might different creative practices speak to each other? How can art collaborate with activist or organizational approaches? Can this help us think more holistically about where to focus and how to proceed? To argue more forcefully for the value of our impractical creations?

And in the spirit of Emma Goldman, how do we ensure there will always be dancing with our revolutions? ■

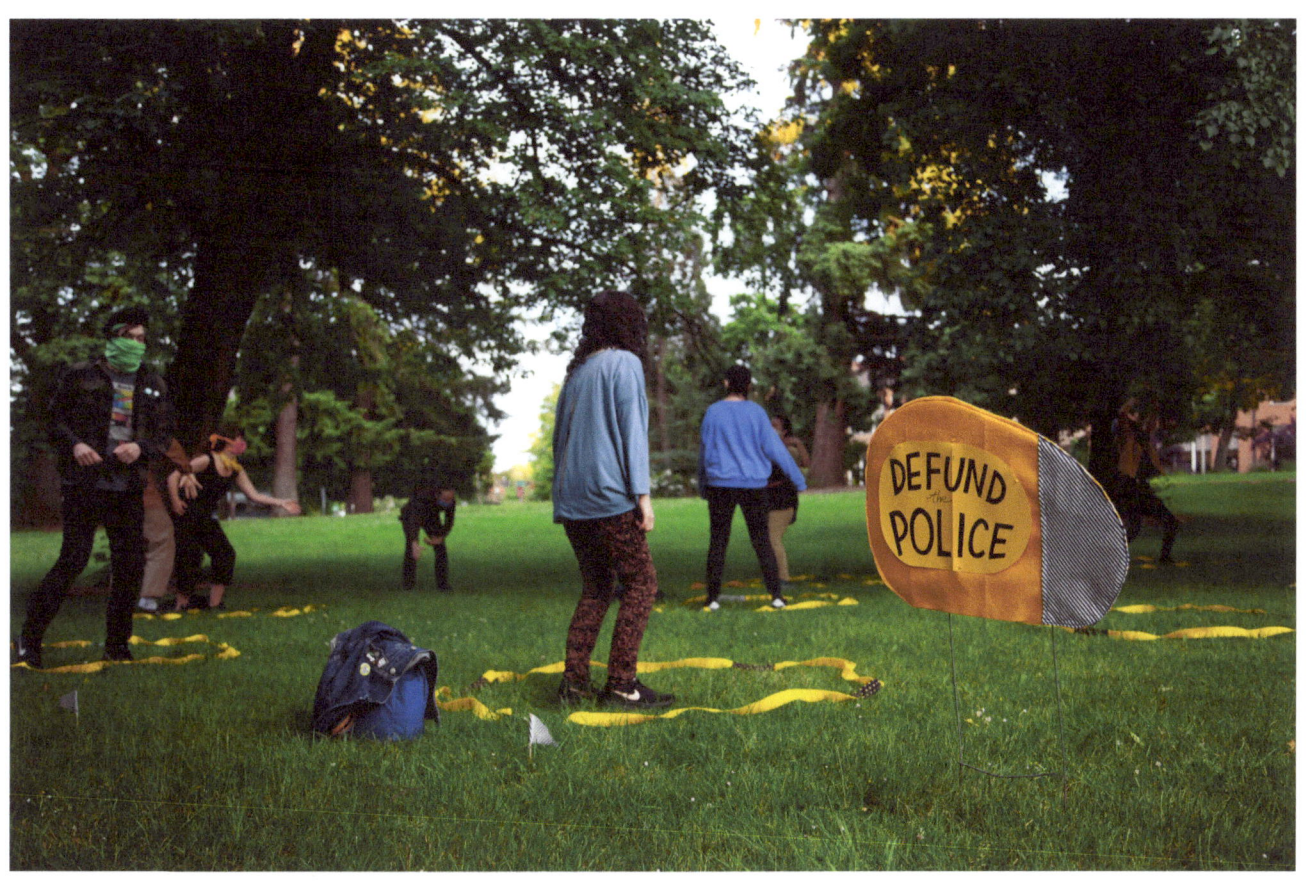
Emergency Dance Party at Alberta Park. Photo by Emily Fitzgerald

THANK YOUS & ADDITIONAL INSPIRATIONS

Community ties provided the greatest resource for manifesting these projects. I want to acknowledge the many people who supported this work.

My fellow students in PSU's Art and Social Practice program: Tia Kramer, Roshani Thakore, Artist Michael Bernard Stevenson Jr, Eric J Olson, Carlos Reynoso, Emma Duehr, Jordan Rosenblum, Nola Hanson, Brianna Ortega, Justin Maxon, Mary Olin Geiger, Rebecca Copper, Illia Yakovenko, and Shelbie Loomis.

My advisors: Harrell Fletcher, Yaelle Amir, Ariana Jacob and Michelle Illuminato, who gave me thoughtful feedback and support

Shawn Creeden, for live sound design on Evacuation Routes

Sarah Farahat aka Seamstress of Sound, for DJing fabulosity on EDPN

Artist Michael Bernard Stevenson Jr, for ground control on EDPN and Evacuation Routes

Many thanks to the people who offered their personal perspectives during my research on disaster: Mo Geiger, Eva Irwin, Ernie Jones, Emma Stocker, Doug Dicharry, JM, MB

Participants' feedback made all of these projects much stronger, especially Sacha Marini, Gretchen Till, Mary Doyle, Tia Factor, Ammi Keller, Anne Williams, Sophie Nathenson

Kirk Rea and City Repair, for bringing the work to fresh audiences

Everybody who sent me audio of pandemic-stilled public spaces: Amanda Boulos, Claude Förster, Damon Reaves, Flavia Tritto, Jacqueline Mabey, Elizabeth Burden, Lucia Novoa Gil, Megan Voeller, Nicolas Grenier, Xi Jie Ng, Shirin Fahimi

Members of the PREPHub committee and emergency management: Kristin Tufte, Ernie Jones, Emma Stocker, Kimberly Howard, Stephen Percy, Sergio Palleroni

Ashara Ekundayo: Artist as First Responder

Kelley Meister: Fallout Shelter

Annie Danger: The Hands That Feed You

Missouri Community Action Network: Poverty Simulation Kit

Mutual Aid Disaster Relief

The situations for a happening should come from what you see in the real world, from real places and people rather than from the head. If you stick to imagination too much you'll end up with old art again, since art was always supposed to be made from imagination. Take advantage of readymade events: a factory fire, the fire trucks screaming to it from all sides, the water, the police barricades, the red blinkers—a natural.
   —Alan Kaprow
     How to Make a Happening

Written, designed and illustrated
by Zeph Fishlyn

zephrocious.com

2nd edition published January 2021

www.ingramcontent.com/pod-product-compliance
Lightning Source LLC
Chambersburg PA
CBHW040058250526
45473CB00044B/2279